LIFE UNPLUGGED

WOMEN'S JOURNAL

CONNECT & SUPPORT

www.lifeunplugged.org

info@lifeunplugged.com

This book was put together by Whitney Beaudoin.

Articles were written by Teri Craft and Debbie Rasa.

Edited by Lindsey Wright

TABLE OF CONTENTS

Intro Process 3

What is SOAP? 6

Initiate 8

The Power of Hope: Harnessing God's Promises to Break Through Stagnation and Embrace Change 12

What's Holding You Back? 15

The Connection Paradox: Managing Technology for Healthy Relationships 20

Cultivate 26

Called To Belong: Building Strong Connections Through Healthy Relationships 30

Nutrients for Growth: A Framework for Relational Health 34

Investigate 36

The Power of Embracing Change 41

Exercise: Values & Priorities 46

Integrate 48

Naming Your Shield: Finding Freedom Through Vulnerability 52

Responding Vs. Reacting: Cultivating Connection in the Face of Instinctual Triggers 56

Blended Families: When Family Extends Beyond Blood 58

Finding Peace in the Present 62

Advocate 64

Beyond Ego: Exploring the Nature of Selflessness in Leadership 68

Good Boundaries: Protecting the Internal & Empowering the External 72

Authentic Leadership 74

Your Story: Serving Others with Your Story 76

INTRO TO WOMEN'S JOURNAL

WRITTEN BY
Teri Craft | Co-Founder of Life Unplugged
Debbie Rasa | Executive Director of Life Unplugged
Lindsey Wright | Wright Copy Co.

Welcome to the Life Unplugged Women's Journal. Our goal is to give you a space to unplug from the noise and distractions of life so you can connect more deeply with God—who He is and all He has for you.

As you begin navigating your way through, we want to inform you that we'll focus on five key elements. Let's break them down so you know what to expect as we embark on this journey together.

Hey! I'm Teri Craft. Let me tell you more about this journey that you are beginning.

(scan to watch)

1 - Initiate

to begin, set, get going, or originate.

Initiating the first step towards growth is always the hardest! That's why we are so glad you are here. Growth is not something that happens passively but rather something you actively pursue. Even better, when you can take a step towards growth and embrace transformation, you often experience the most progress. As you set off on this journey, we first want to consider what it means to initiate growth.

Take some time to consider:

- In what areas am I feeling stuck? What's holding me back?
- Ask someone close to you if they see any blind spots you may not be aware of in your life.

_____

_____

_____

_____

_____

_____

_____

_____

_____

2 - Cultivate

to promote the growth and development of one's life.

"Two are better than one because they have a good return for their labor: If either of them falls down, one can help the other up. But pity anyone who falls and has no one to help them up. Also, if two lie down together, they will keep warm. But how can one keep warm alone? Though one may be overpowered, two can defend themselves. A cord of three strands is not quickly broken."
Ecclesiastes 4:9-12

A huge focus of this journal is the importance of cultivating relationships. We were never meant to walk through life alone. As women, we are often naturally bent towards relationships. But that doesn't mean we know how to engage with relationships healthily. Throughout our journey, we'll explore the value of deep, connected relationships and how to cultivate authenticity, honesty, and accountability. We need one another to get the relational nutrients essential to our humanity, especially our growth. We will consider how you can foster a community that will aid in your growth — and the growth of others!

Take time to consider:

- Do you have any relational wounds that need tending?
- Take inventory of the authenticity of your relationships.
- With whom do you want to cultivate a more profound connection?

_____

_____

_____

_____

_____

_____

3 - Investigate

examine; to search out particulars; to learn the facts about something hidden.

Curiosity is one of the greatest tools for growth. A lack of curiosity leads to stagnation, judgment, and often fear. But an openness to investigating what you don't know expands your understanding, perspective, and, ultimately, your capacity for growth. A posture of humility and a willingness to investigate are crucial in the growth journey.

Take time to consider:

- What have I stopped being curious about? Why?
- What am I curious about right now?
- What makes me feel most alive?

_____

_____

_____

_____

4 - Integrate

to bring together or incorporate parts – both good and bad – into a whole.

As you embark on this journey of growth, the integration process will lead to true transformation. We must take what we learn and apply it to our lives. Integration is the process of weaving together our head knowledge, our heart knowledge, and our life choices. When we seek to integrate what we are learning into our lives, we can live with congruence – where our values align with our choices. That's the path toward authenticity and peace!

Take time to consider:

- What painful experiences do I need to integrate into my life?
- What keeps me from integrating all parts of my life – the good and the bad?
- Imagine your life with authenticity and integration.

_____

_____

_____

5 - Advocate

intercessor; one who stands on behalf of another; supporter.

"'Teacher, which is the greatest commandment in the Law?' Jesus replied: 'Love the Lord your God with all your heart and with all your soul and with all your mind. This is the first and greatest commandment. And the second is like it: Love your neighbor as yourself. All the Law and the Prophets hang on these two commandments.'"
Matthew 22:36-40

The Great Commandment reminds us to love God and grow in our relationship with Him and ourselves, as well as love others as ourselves. To do this authentically, we need to take time to honestly assess our limits and wounds and then take steps towards healing and growth. The culmination of our journey together is taking on a posture of serving, advocating for, and supporting others. Our advocacy is the legacy we leave for others.

Take time to consider:

- Is it more difficult for me to love myself or others? Why?
- What has hindered my ability to authentically advocate for and serve others?
- What do I want my legacy to be?

_____

_____

_____

_____

_____

_____

_____

_____

_____

_____

We are excited that you have taken this step to journey through the Life Unplugged Women's Journal to move towards growth and transformation. As you embark, we hope you remember that **you are not alone!**

Let's begin.

WHAT ARE SOAP DEVOTIONS?

SOAP is a simple method for reading and applying God's Word to our lives. SOAP stands for Scripture, Observation, Application, and Prayer. With these four steps, you can learn to enjoy daily devotions with God and firmly plant His Word in your heart:

1. *Scripture* – As you read God's Word, write down a portion that stands out. According to the Learning Center at UNC, "Writing [versus typing] appears to help us more deeply encode information that we're trying to learn because there is a direct connection between our hand and our brain."

2. *Observation* – After writing down the scripture verse(s), sit with it briefly, and then write your observation of that scripture.

3. *Application* – After writing your observation, this is the time you want to apply it to your life personally. What practical message does the scripture hold for you?

4. *Prayer* – Write a prayer to the Lord after the previous three steps. Ask Him to help you live this scripture out in your life.

As you can see, by using this simple but effective process, you will grow in knowledge and understanding of God's Word. You cannot live as the person God intended you to be unless you allow God's Word to influence, empower, instruct, and guide you every step of the way. Here is a sample SOAP journal entry:

More about SOAP from Wayne Cordeiro
(scan to watch)

Here is a sample SOAP journal entry:

Scripture
"Two are better than one because they have a good return for their labor: If either of them falls down, one can help the other up. But pity anyone who falls and has no one to help them up. Also, if two lie down together, they will keep warm. But how can one keep warm alone? Though one may be overpowered, two can defend themselves. A cord of three strands is not quickly broken."

Ecclesiastes 4:9-12

Observation
There are many benefits to being with others. We can get more work done, be lifted when we fall, and keep one another warm. When I'm with others, I'm not easily overpowered or broken. There is wisdom in being connected with others.

Application
Even though I love being in relationships with others, I often shield them from seeing when I am in need. I am tempted to believe that I should be able to do everything on my own, and that friendship is just for the joy of it. It's hard for me to ask for help. But I also realize that I feel honored when I am able to be there for others. I need to let others be there for me, too.

Prayer
Please forgive me for the times I have isolated and pushed others away. I know you are calling me to let my guard down and be vulnerable with a few people I can trust. Please help me see my pride and fear whenever I start hiding from the people I claim to be close to. Please help me to let them in and trust that you use relationships to strengthen, encourage, and lift me up.

NOW IT'S YOUR TURN TO TRY IT OUT.

(scan to start)

INIT

ATE

Let me tell you more about this
section, "INITIATE."

(scan to watch)

SOAP DEVOTIONS

Scripture

"Jesus called them together and said, 'You know that the rulers of the Gentiles lord it over them, and their high officials exercise authority over them. Not so with you. Instead, whoever wants to become great among you must be your servant, and whoever wants to be first must be your slave—just as the Son of Man did not come to be served, but to serve and to give his life as a ransom for many.'"

Matthew 20:25-28

Application

Observation

Prayer

THE POWER OF HOPE:
Harnessing God's Promises to Break Through Stagnation and Embrace Change

Stagnation can be a formidable force, trapping us in a state of complacency and hindering our growth. However, as believers, we have access to a powerful source of transformation and renewal: hope in God's promises. This article will explore the acronym HOPE from a biblical perspective, understanding how it empowers us to break through stagnation, embrace change, and experience the abundant life God intends for us.

H - Holding onto God's Faithfulness

Our hope is grounded in God's faithfulness. Throughout the pages of scripture, we witness His unwavering commitment to His people. By holding onto His faithfulness, we are reminded that He is always working on our behalf, even in the midst of stagnation. We can trust that His plans for us are good and that He will lead us into a season of transformation and growth.

WHERE IN YOUR LIFE DO YOU NEED TO LET GO OF CONTROL?

_____

_____

WHERE HAS GOD BEEN FAITHFUL IN YOUR LIFE?

_____

_____

WHERE HAVE YOU BEEN STAGNANT IN YOUR LIFE?

_____

_____

O - Overcoming Fear and Doubt

Fear and doubt often paralyze us, preventing us from embracing change. However, with hope in God, we can overcome these obstacles. The Bible reassures us that God has not given us a spirit of fear, but of power, love, and a sound mind (2 Timothy 1:7). As we place our hope in Him, we find the courage to step out of our comfort zones, trusting that He will guide us through every transition.

WHERE HAS FEAR AND DOUBT PARALYZED YOU IN YOUR LIFE?

_____

_____

WHERE IN YOUR LIFE DOES GOD WANT YOU TO STEP OUT AND TRUST HIM?

_____

_____

P - Promises of Renewal and Restoration

God's promises bring hope for renewal and restoration in our lives. Scriptures like Isaiah 43:19 remind us that God is constantly at work, making a way in the wilderness and bringing us to streams in the desert. When we feel stuck or stagnant, we can hold onto these promises, knowing that God can transform even the most challenging situations. He can breathe new life into our circumstances, leading us into a season of positive change.

WHERE DO YOU FEEL DRIED UP IN LIFE?

_____

_____

WHAT ARE YOU FACING IN LIFE THAT FEELS IMPOSSIBLE?

_____

_____

WHAT POSITIVE CHANGE DO YOU NEED RIGHT NOW?

_____

_____

E - Embracing God's Perfect Timing

Embracing change requires patience and trust in God's perfect timing. Ecclesiastes 3:1 reminds us that there is a season for everything under the sun. When we feel stuck or impatient, we can find hope in the knowledge that God is orchestrating the events of our lives for our ultimate good. He knows the perfect time to release us from stagnation and lead us into new opportunities for growth and transformation.

WHERE DO YOU FEEL YOU ARE RUNNING OUT OF TIME AND NEED A MIRACLE?

_____

_____

WHAT IS HOLDING YOU BACK FROM TRUSTING GOD IN YOUR SITUATION?

_____

_____

As believers, we are not called to live in stagnation but to embrace the power of hope in God's promises. By holding onto His faithfulness, overcoming fear and doubt, embracing His promises of renewal and restoration, and trusting in His perfect timing, we can break through stagnation and fully embrace the change God has in store for us. Let us anchor our hope in Him, allowing His transformative power to guide us into a season of growth, purpose, and abundant life.

CONSIDERING HOPE, WRITE A PRAYER TO GOD, ASKING HIM TO HELP YOU TRUST HIM AS HE LEADS YOU.

_____

_____

_____

WHAT'S HOLDING YOU BACK?

by Teri Craft

Have you ever felt like there needs to be more time in the day to do everything you want (or need) to do? Truthfully, as women, there really aren't enough hours to cross everything off our daily list. If we spend all of our time and energy focusing on getting everything done, we will struggle to be present from moment to moment. In this article, we want to recognize your responsibilities and the many plates you're working tirelessly to keep spinning. So many people and things in your life depend on you. It's not in your head. And it feels like too much because it is too much.

I wish we could pause time, hire a team to complete every task on your list, and let you enjoy a spa retreat while it's all taken care of! And you can do that from time to time! But, as you well know, life's day-to-day does not stop. And we know that you feel it—because we do, too!

That's why we won't give you a formula for allocating your time better or a hack for mastering your schedule and to-do list. Instead, we invite you to consider the areas of your life where you can have the most significant impact.

We don't think your calendar, to-do list, or limitations are the enemy. But we do believe there is a way to identify what is most important to you and shift your focus accordingly. In this article, we will invite you to take time each day to ground yourself in what matters most— letting that guide how you go about your day rather than letting it overwhelm your full plate or shame you for not doing it perfectly.

Let's consider the areas of your life where you are uniquely positioned to have an impact that only you can create.

Only you can ...

Be the wife to your husband
Be the mother to your children
Grow your relationship with Christ
Care for your body
Enjoy your life

Let's look at these five areas where only you can create an impact.

1 Only you can be the wife to your husband.

If you are married, your spouse is among your most sacred and significant relationships. And yet, we are so prone to go into autopilot within marriage, especially when life piles up with work, the house, kids, or health concerns. It's also natural to put up walls in your marriage if you've been hurt, rejected, or disappointed. And yet, only you (along with your spouse) can cultivate a flourishing marriage. It takes intention. It takes desire. It takes work. And when you put in the effort to prioritize your marriage, it impacts all other areas of your life. Consider how you can move towards your spouse today. It could be as simple as a quick check-in where you look them in the eyes, offer touch, and listen to how they are doing. Maybe it's considering him when you're at the store, and you remember to snag his favorite snack. Or maybe your marriage needs something a little more. The point is to remember that your marriage matters. And it won't flourish without your care and attention.

Here is some good advice: stick with your wife! You may have made mistakes in your past, but you can make choices to change. You can move toward repentance, recovery, and restoration. You can choose to be faithful and invested with your wife from here on out.

2 Only you can be the mom to your kids.

If you are a mom, this one is likely easy for you to remember. Their needs are many, they're not shy about making them known, and you are often their primary source for meeting them! The reminder about your role in their life isn't meant to add pressure to what you likely already feel. Instead, it's to assure you that you matter. And no one can replace the role you play in their lives. Regardless of how much time they spend at school or with other caretakers, you will always be their safest place.

One of the best things you can do for your kids is to model how to care for yourself even as you care for others. They will learn so much from watching you. At times, you may feel like the maid, the cook, and the manager of all the things, but remember that more than any of those things, you are their mother. They need you – simply your presence – above all else. Consider how you can delegate the tasks that overwhelm you. As your kids grow (even starting at a young age!), begin inviting them to come alongside you in the daily tasks required to run the household. Not only will it ease your burden over time, but it'll foster a closeness with them, rather than frantically doing everything yourself while they do their own thing.

In the times when you feel overwhelmed, discouraged, or frustrated, know that you are doing sacred work as a mom. And it isn't easy. It's one of the most challenging roles in life. Find people who can say "me too" about the hard stuff and offer a listening ear when you just need to vent. Seek out older women with perspective and insight into your season. And remember that motherhood is not something you ever complete. You will make mistakes. You will fail yourself and your children. And you will get to show them how to repair relationships, seek and offer grace, and seek the Lord in all things.

3 Only you can grow your relationship with Christ.

Only you can foster growth in your relationship with Jesus. Not even the best sermon, book, or devotional guide can do this work for you. You have to be the one to turn to Him when you're weary, share your feelings with Him when you're overwhelmed, and process with Him when you're confused. No one else can spend time with Him. No one else can share your heart with Him. And no one else can receive His love into your spirit for you.

But none of it has to be as complicated as we often make it. Growing your relationship with Jesus can look like talking aloud to Him whenever you're alone in the car. Or playing worship music as you complete household tasks. Or listening to a podcast, an audiobook, or simply Scripture read aloud as you take a walk on a mid-day break. He wants to connect with you. And the beauty of a relationship with Him is that He is both perfect and full of grace. He won't let you down, leave you hanging, or say the wrong thing. He knows you perfectly and offers unconditional love and judgment-free adoration. Being in a relationship with Him is a healing balm to our often parched, discouraged, and frustrated hearts. *He alone can offer* the fullness of what you need. And you alone can accept that from Him.

4 Only you can care for your body.

Things can feel complicated when it comes to our bodies, especially as women in our culture. Often, we vacillate between neglecting our bodies and obsessing over them – ridden with self-contempt or tempted by vanity. While our culture has made strides toward body positivity and body neutrality, Scripture gives us the most clear perspective on how to approach our bodies. There is not one magical verse but rather the overall message of God's Word that compels us to care for our bodies as temples through which we love, serve, and connect with God.

Caring for your body can involve movement and nourishing foods, but it can also involve grounding practices and paying attention to your body's signals. It consists of listening to the information that your emotions signal to you. It involves allowing your body to feel and process emotions rather than stifle, suppress, or overanalyze them.

Caring for your body is holy work. And you are the only one who can take care of your one and only body. We pray that you have the grace to accept your body's gifts and the discipline to make choices that will strengthen, nourish, and heal your body.

5 Only you can enjoy your life.

When you live with an intention to enjoy life, you cultivate an appreciation for God and all He has given you! You're also fulfilling the purpose He created you to live: to enjoy life!

"So here is what you should do: go and enjoy your meals, drink your wine, and love every minute of it because God is already pleased with what you do. Dress your best, and don't forget a splash of scented fragrance. Enjoy life with the woman you love. Cherish every moment of the fleeting life God has given you under the sun." Ecclesiastes 9:7-9 (The Voice)

If you've read Ecclesiastes, you know that this passage follows a prolonged, meandering existential crisis in which King Solomon questions the meaning of life. He has access to all the pleasures of life, yet he sees how transient everything is. Nothing lasts forever. Everything comes and goes. In the end, he's left with a simple truth: **all we can do in this life is enjoy the gifts we've been given.**

What are some ways you can practice this? Here are some ideas:

- Take a deep breath and savor all the goodness of the present moment.
- Take time to enjoy your food.
- Take time to have fun with a friend.
- Take time to delight in and play with your child.
- Take time to savor the sunrise.

When you intentionally enjoy your life, you multiply the goodness it offers!

Take advantage of this one!

REFLECTION

What is overwhelming you right now?

_____

_____

_____

_____

Which of the 5 things only you can do is most challenging for you to prioritize? Which is easiest?

_____

_____

_____

_____

What would it look like for you to integrate these priorities into your life?

_____

_____

_____

_____

What's one change you can make right now to begin prioritizing what matters most?

_____

_____

_____

_____

MANAGING TECHNOLOGY FOR HEALTHY RELATIONSHIPS

In today's digital age, technology has transformed how we interact, communicate, and form relationships. While technological advancements have undeniably enhanced our lives in numerous ways, they have also created a paradox: The more connected we are through devices, the more disconnected we feel from authentic human interaction.

Percent U.S. Anxiety Prevalence

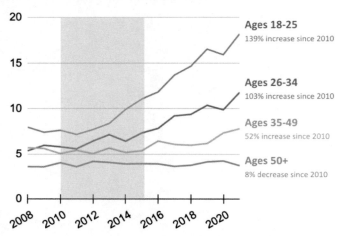

Ages 18-25
139% increase since 2010

Ages 26-34
103% increase since 2010

Ages 35-49
52% increase since 2010

Ages 50+
8% decrease since 2010

SOURCE: U.S. National Survey on Drug Use and Health

HOW DO YOU SEE THESE PLAYING OUT IN YOUR LIFE?

_____

_____

_____

The Impact of Technology on Relationships

The proliferation of smartphones, social media platforms, and digital communication has significantly changed the landscape of relationships. According to a study by the Pew Research Center, around 81% of Americans own a smartphone, and nearly 72% use some form of social media. While these technologies have made staying in touch with others more accessible, they have also given rise to concerning trends.

1. **Decline in Face-to-Face Interaction:** The increased reliance on digital communication has reduced face-to-face interactions. People are more likely to send a text message or chat online than meet in person, leading to a decline in the depth and quality of relationships. Time spent on social media can also consume our time, preventing us from meaningful in-person interactions.
2. **Communication Misinterpretations:** Text-based communication lacks the nuances of verbal and non-verbal cues, leading to misunderstandings and misinterpretations, potentially causing conflict and distancing people emotionally.
3. **Social Media and Anxiety:** Research is beginning to show a clear correlation between social media use and anxiety. This is especially true among adolescents, and particularly so for girls. The rise of phone use among children has led to sleep deprivation, social deprivation, attention fragmentation, and addiction.
4. **Parent-Child Disconnect:** Technology, especially smartphones, can interfere with parent-child interactions, as parents may become engrossed in their devices instead of fully engaging with their children. Furthermore, our children mimic what we model. When they begin using their own devices, if they do not have appropriate boundaries (as modeled by their parents), it can increase the difficulty of connecting with them.

The Role of Mothers: Modeling Healthy Connections and Boundaries

Mothers have arguably the most influential role in their children's lives. From an early age, they have the most influence on shaping their kids' values, teaching them right from wrong, and modeling how to care for themselves and treat others. That same influence translates to the particularly profound impact mothers can have on the trajectory of their kids' relationship with technology.

When we are distracted by screens and social media, our children not only feel the disconnection from us but also learn how to use screens in their lives. We recognize that technology is a part of our daily lives. And for many, if not most, of us, technology plays a vital role in our work. It's OK for our children to see us using technology. What's important is that we remain aware of our use of technology, when it may be distracting us from the present, and when we may need to set boundaries for our health as a model of healthy technology use for our children.

Practical Ways to Manage Technology and Prioritize Healthy Relationships

1. **Set Boundaries**: Establish technology-free zones and times, especially during family meals and bedtime. Create a culture where being fully present with family takes precedence over the digital world.
2. **Be an Active Listener:** When communicating with your children, actively listen. Put away devices, maintain eye contact, and show genuine interest in what they have to say.
3. **Lead by Example:** Demonstrate healthy technology habits to your children. If you expect them to limit screen time, you must first model it in your own life.
4. **Engage in Shared Activities:** Find activities you and your children enjoy and participate in together. Whether it's playing games, reading books, or cooking together, shared experiences foster stronger bonds.
5. **Promote Outdoor Time:** Encourage outdoor play and exploration. Nature provides an excellent environment for connection and bonding.
6. **Communicate Openly:** Have regular conversations about the benefits and downsides of technology. Teach your kids to be responsible digital citizens and guide them in using technology mindfully.

While technology has undoubtedly transformed our lives, it is essential to recognize the potential harm it can cause to our relationships—especially the connection between parents and their children. By being mindful of our technology usage and prioritizing human interaction, we can strike a balance that allows healthy relationships to flourish in the digital age. As parents, embracing this approach will lead to stronger connections with our kids and foster their emotional growth and well-being.

HOW WOULD YOU DESCRIBE YOUR CURRENT RELATIONSHIP WITH TECHNOLOGY?

HOW WILL YOU COMMIT TO MANAGING TECHNOLOGY TO PRIORITIZE HEALTHY RELATIONSHIPS?

Scripture

"Not neglecting to meet together, as is the habit of some, but encouraging one another, and all the more as you see the Day drawing near."

Hebrews 10:25

SOAP DEVOTIONS

Observation

Application

Prayer

CULT

VATE

Let me tell you more about this section, "CULTIVATE."
(scan to watch)

Scripture

"As iron sharpens iron,
so a friend sharpens a friend."

Proverbs 27:17

SOAP DEVOTIONS

Observation

_____
_____
_____
_____
_____
_____

Application

_____
_____
_____
_____
_____
_____
_____

Prayer

_____
_____
_____
_____
_____
_____
_____

Called to Belong:
BUILDING STRONG CONNECTIONS THROUGH HEALTHY RELATIONSHIPS

We were never meant to live alone. You've likely heard it noted before, but the first and only time that God said something was not good in the creation story was after He had created Adam and before He had created Eve.

"God said, 'It's not good for the Man to be alone; I'll make him a helper, a companion."
Genesis 2:18

While this passage may specifically refer to men and women, the whole of Scripture reveals that it's much more about our human need for companionship, relationships, and community.

Later, when the early Church was established after Jesus's resurrection, the beauty of community, connection, and belonging took on new life.

"And they devoted themselves to the apostles' teaching and the fellowship, to the breaking of bread and the prayers. And awe came upon every soul, and many wonders and signs were being done through the apostles. And all who believed were together and had all things in common. And they were selling their possessions and belongings and distributing the proceeds to all, as any had need. And day by day, attending the temple together and breaking bread in their homes, they received their food with glad and generous hearts, praising God and having favor with all the people. And the Lord added to their number day by day those who were being saved."
Acts 2:42-47

Fast-forward 2,000+ years, and there are so many barriers to living connected lives marked by belonging. Our individualistic, technology-driven culture is set up for isolation. Most of us spend most of our days at our own desks, in our own cars, and in our own homes. It requires profound intention and immense effort to break out of isolation and forge a real community. And yet, this kind of authentic connectedness is imperative for our health and our growth.

Author and speaker Jennie Allen had this to say about our current state in her book Find Your People: "We've replaced intrusive, real conversations with small talk, and we've substituted soul-baring, deep, connected living with texts and a night out together every once in a while." She shares, "I'd reveal enough so people felt close to me but not give anyone enough to use against me." And isn't that just so real? Listen, it is not wise to bear your soul to every person you meet. Or even every Christian friend. But it is wise to have a select few with full access to know and speak to all of you. That's how we tangibly experience the kind of love that Jesus offers. The kind that says, "I see you — good and bad — and I love you." That kind of relationship provides the ongoing healing we need as we move through this world.

Neuroscientist and author Curt Thompson has much to say about this in his book Anatomy of the Soul. "Our Western world has long emphasized knowledge—factual information and 'proof'—over the process of being known by God and others. No wonder, then, that despite all our technological advancements and the proliferation of social media, we are more intra- and interpersonally isolated than ever. Yet it is only when we are known that we are positioned to become conduits of love. And it is love that transforms our minds, makes forgiveness possible, and weaves a community of disparate people into the tapestry of God's family."

WHAT RESONATES MOST WITH YOU FROM THESE PASSAGES ABOVE?

_____

_____

_____

_____

_____

IS THERE ANYONE WITH WHOM YOU ARE FULLY KNOWN? IF YES, WHAT HAS THAT BEEN LIKE FOR YOU? IF NOT, WHAT KEEPS YOU FROM IT, AND WITH WHOM COULD YOU BEGIN TO OPEN UP MORE FULLY?

_____

_____

_____

_____

_____

IS THERE ANYONE IN YOUR LIFE TO WHOM YOU COULD OFFER BELONGING?

_____

_____

_____

_____

_____

WHAT PRACTICAL WAY CAN YOU REACH OUT TO SOMEONE THIS WEEK TO FOSTER A MORE PROFOUND CONNECTION?

_____

_____

_____

_____

_____

TWO ARE
better than one!

In Leadership Magazine, Carl Connor writes about the dangers of standing alone. A few winters ago, heavy snow hit North Carolina. Following a wet, six-inch snowfall, it was interesting to see the effect along I-40. Next to the highway stood several large groves of tall, young pine trees. The branches were bowed down with heavy snow – so low that branches from one tree often leaned against the trunk of the branches of another. Where trees stood alone, however, the effect of the heavy snow was different. The branches became heavier and heavier, bearing the weight of the snow alone. Since there were no other trees to lean against or help support the weight of the snow, the branches of these trees snapped. They lay on the ground, buried, dark, and alone in the cold snow.

When the storms of life hit, we need to be standing close to others. We need each other, because we can't bear the full weight of the hard times in life on our own. The closer we stand in community, the more we will be able to hold up – throughout our lives and especially during tough times.

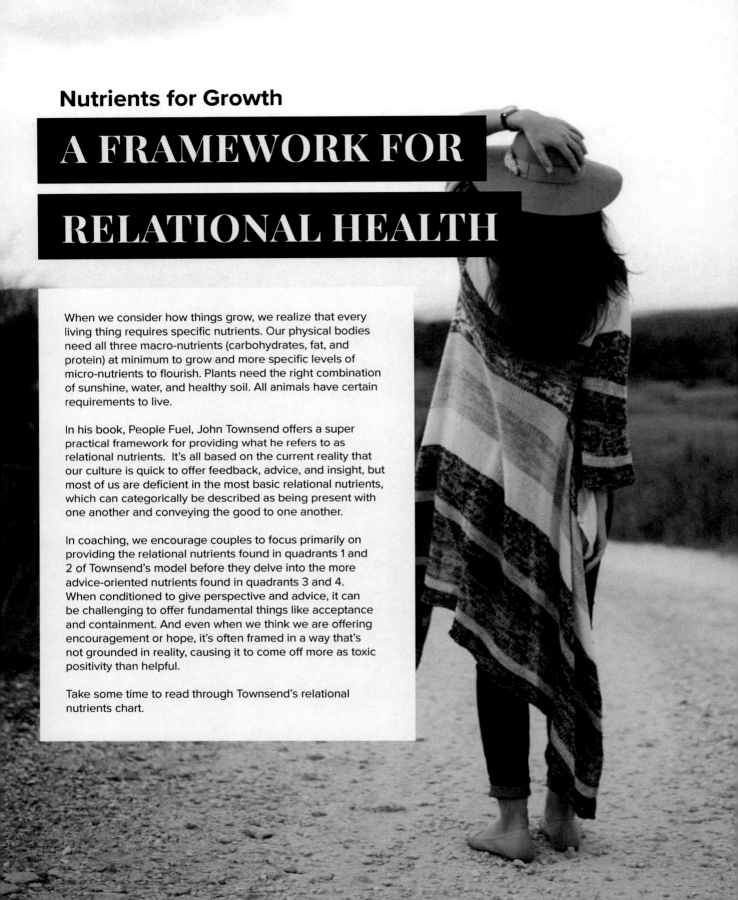

Nutrients for Growth

A FRAMEWORK FOR

RELATIONAL HEALTH

When we consider how things grow, we realize that every living thing requires specific nutrients. Our physical bodies need all three macro-nutrients (carbohydrates, fat, and protein) at minimum to grow and more specific levels of micro-nutrients to flourish. Plants need the right combination of sunshine, water, and healthy soil. All animals have certain requirements to live.

In his book, People Fuel, John Townsend offers a super practical framework for providing what he refers to as relational nutrients. It's all based on the current reality that our culture is quick to offer feedback, advice, and insight, but most of us are deficient in the most basic relational nutrients, which can categorically be described as being present with one another and conveying the good to one another.

In coaching, we encourage couples to focus primarily on providing the relational nutrients found in quadrants 1 and 2 of Townsend's model before they delve into the more advice-oriented nutrients found in quadrants 3 and 4. When conditioned to give perspective and advice, it can be challenging to offer fundamental things like acceptance and containment. And even when we think we are offering encouragement or hope, it's often framed in a way that's not grounded in reality, causing it to come off more as toxic positivity than helpful.

Take some time to read through Townsend's relational nutrients chart.

WHAT STANDS OUT TO YOU?

_____

_____

_____

_____

WHICH OF THE NUTRIENTS DO YOU TEND TO GIVE TO OTHERS?

_____

_____

_____

_____

WHICH NUTRIENTS DO YOU NEED RIGHT NOW? CONSIDER FOCUSING ON QUADRANTS 1 AND 2 BEFORE YOU DELVE INTO QUADRANTS 3 AND 4.

_____

_____

_____

_____

WHO CAN YOU ASK TO MEET THESE RELATIONAL NEEDS THIS WEEK?

_____

_____

_____

_____

WHAT WOULD IT LOOK LIKE TO PHYSICALLY USE THIS CHART AS A REFERENCE THE NEXT TIME YOU NEED CONNECTION? HOW CAN YOU INVITE SOMEONE ELSE TO USE IT WITH YOU?

_____

_____

_____

_____

We are better together!

1 QUADRANT 1
BE PRESENT

ACCEPTANCE
Connect without judgment.

IDENTIFICATION
Share your similar story.

ATTUNEMENT
Respond to what another is experiencing. Get "in their well."

CONTAINMENT
Allow the other to vent while staying warm without reacting.

VALIDATION
Convey that person's experience is significant and not to be dismissed.

COMFORT
Provide support for someone's loss.

2 QUADRANT 2
CONVEY THE GOOD

AFFIRMATION
Draw attention to the good.

HOPE
Provide reality-based confidence in the future.

ENCOURAGEMENT
Convey that you believe in someone's ability to do the difficult.

FORGIVENESS
Cancel a debt.

RESPECT
Assign value.

CELEBRATION
Acknowledge a win, both cognitively and emotionally.

3 QUADRANT 3
PROVIDE REALITY

CLARIFICATION
Bring order to confusion.

FEEDBACK
Give a personal response.

PERSPECTIVE
Offer a different viewpoint.

CONFRONTATION
Face someone with an appeal to change.

INSIGHT
Convey a deeper understanding.

4 QUADRANT 4
CALL TO ACTION

ADVICE
Recommend an action step.

DEVELOPMENT
Create a growth environment.

STRUCTURE
Provide a framework.

SERVICE
Guide engagement to giving back.

CHALLENGE
Strongly recommend a difficult action.

INVEST

TIGATE

Let me tell you more about section, "INVESTIGATE."
(scan to watch)

SOAP DEVOTIONS

Scripture

"Search me, O God, and know my heart; test me and know my anxious thoughts. Point out anything in me that offends you, and lead me along the path of everlasting life."

Psalm 139:23-24 (NLT)

Application

Observation

Prayer

THE POWER OF EMBRACING CHANGE

Change is an inherent part of life. It is a force that shapes and transforms us, propelling us toward growth, discovery, and new possibilities. It empowers us to break free from stagnation, discover our hidden potential, and navigate life's challenges with resilience. Embracing change enables us to evolve, learn, and discover new opportunities that lead to a more fulfilling and purposeful existence.

Let's explore the power of embracing change and how it can lead to personal and collective transformation.

1. Embracing the Unpredictability of Change: Change is often accompanied by uncertainty and the unknown. While this can be unsettling, it is essential to recognize that tremendous potential lies within that unpredictability. When we embrace change, we open ourselves up to new experiences, opportunities, and perspectives that can enrich our lives.

"In their hearts humans plan their course, but the Lord establishes their steps." **Proverbs 16:9 (NIV)**

We tend to make plans and set our course, but Proverbs reminds us that, ultimately, the Lord determines our steps. Wisdom encourages us to embrace the unpredictability of change, trusting that God's guidance and sovereignty are at work in our lives.

WHERE ARE YOU IN THE MIDST OF CHANGE RIGHT NOW? HOW CAN YOU EMBRACE THE UNPREDICTABILITY OF IT?

_____

_____

_____

2. Embracing the Catalyst of Change: Change challenges us to step out of our comfort zones and confront our limitations. It pushes us to develop new skills, adapt to different situations, and expand our horizons. We discover our inner strength and resilience through change, unlocking untapped potential and facilitating personal growth.

"And we all, who with unveiled faces contemplate the Lord's glory, are being transformed into his image with ever-increasing glory, which comes from the Lord, who is the Spirit." **2 Corinthians 3:18 (NIV)**

This scripture highlights that as we behold the glory of the Lord, we are transformed into His likeness. Change becomes a catalyst for personal growth as we continuously seek Him, allowing His Spirit to mold and shape us into who He intends us to be.

HOW HAS CHANGE BEEN A CATALYST FOR PERSONAL GROWTH IN YOUR LIFE?

_____

_____

_____

_____

3. Embracing the Disruption of Change: Stagnation is the enemy of progress and fulfillment. When we resist change, we become stagnant — trapped in repetitive patterns that hinder our development. However, by embracing change, we break free from the shackles of complacency, allowing ourselves to evolve, explore new avenues, and unleash our creativity.

"Therefore, if anyone is in Christ, the new creation has come; the old has gone, the new is here!" **2 Corinthians 5:17 (NIV)**

This verse emphasizes that when we are in Christ, we are transformed into a new creation. The old ways, habits, and patterns of stagnation are replaced by the power of God's grace and the possibility of a fresh start. Resistance is usually caused by wounds that have created defense mechanisms (adaptive strategies for protection). In our experience, we've found that the enemy will often wound you at your most extraordinary giftedness. When you identify the origin of the wound, you see where you can change your relationship with the "protector" in your life. This is where freedom is found.

IDENTIFY WHERE YOU HAVE BEEN WOUNDED AND BECOME STAGNANT ON YOUR JOURNEY.

_____

_____

_____

_____

4. Embracing the Constance of Change: The world around us constantly evolves, and change is an integral part of its fabric. Those who embrace the constant nature of change are better equipped to navigate the shifting tides of life. By being adaptable, we become more resilient and capable of adjusting our course and seizing opportunities that come our way.

"Jesus Christ is the same yesterday and today and forever." **Hebrews 13:8 (NIV)**

While not directly addressing the concept of change, this verse reminds us of Jesus' unchanging nature. Our foundation in Christ remains secure in an ever-changing world where circumstances and situations constantly shift. Through our relationship with Him, we find the stability, guidance, and strength to navigate the changes around and within us.

WHERE IN YOUR LIFE HAVE YOU BECOME UNTETHERED FROM JESUS AND THE STABILITY HE OFFERS?

_____

_____

_____

_____

5. Embracing the Innovation of Change: An openness to change drives innovation and progress. We create an environment that nurtures creativity and ingenuity when we embrace change. Change encourages us to challenge the status quo, think outside the box, and explore innovative solutions to our problems. Through change, we pave the way for progress and positively impact the world.

WHERE HAVE YOU BEEN INNOVATIVE? IF YOU HAVE STRUGGLED WITH INNOVATION, WHAT HOLDS YOU BACK?

_____

_____

_____

_____

6. Embracing the Inspiration of Change: When we embody the power of change, we become catalysts for transformation in others' lives. Our willingness to embrace change can inspire those around us to do the same. By sharing our experiences, supporting others through their journey of change, and leading by example, we become agents of positive influence and impact in our families and beyond.

"In the same way, let your light shine before others, that they may see your good deeds and glorify your Father in heaven." **Matthew 5:16 (NIV)**

This verse reminds us that our actions, influenced by the positive change that God has done in our lives, can inspire and influence others. When we embrace change and allow it to transform us, our lives testify to God's work in us. This, in turn, can inspire others to seek change in their own lives and ultimately bring glory to God.

WHAT CHANGE HAS GOD DONE IN YOUR LIFE THAT OTHERS NEED TO HEAR ABOUT?

_____

_____

_____

_____

Change is not something to be feared or resisted but embraced and harnessed. It holds within it the power to shape us into the best versions of ourselves, ignite our passions, and unlock our true potential. As we navigate life's ever-changing landscape, let us embrace the power of change, knowing that it can transform us, our relationships, and our world. Remember, change is not a destination but a continuous journey. Embrace, learn from, and let it propel you toward a future filled with growth, fulfillment, and endless possibilities.

To break free from stagnation, you must let go.

Exercise:

VALUES & PRIORITIES

Values: core principles that do not change
Priorities: something of importance that can change depending on external factors

One of the most foundational pieces of living a life of intentional growth is naming your values and aligning your priorities with them. When our choices align with our values, we have a sense of congruence and peace as we move through life. But when we don't consider our values as we prioritize our lives, we experience friction and discord. For most people, it's not simply a matter of aligning your priorities with your values. First, you must reflect and name your values. That's what we want you to do here. List out what you value most in life. Get specific with your life values. The more they resonate with you, the more likely you'll prioritize them in your life.

On the next page, we invite you to take an honest inventory of your current priorities and consider how you may need to shift them.

"But seek first the kingdom of God and his righteousness, and all these things will be added to you." **Matthew 6:33**

Examples:

Value: Quality time with my spouse
Priority: Weekly date nights

Value: Growing in my relationship with Christ
Priority: Daily devotional time

Value: Taking care of my body
Priority: Workout 3x each week

Value: Integrity and honesty
Priority: Sharing vulnerably with community and showing up as my authentic self in all spaces.

Value: Personal growth
Priority: Read for 15 min each night

My Values

1.
2.
3.
4.
5.
6.
7.
8.

My current Priorities

1.
2.
3.
4.
5.

Aligned Priorities

1.
2.
3.
4.
5.

INTE

GRATE

Let me tell you more about this section, **"INTEGRATE."**

(scan to watch)

Scripture

"Do not be conformed to this world, but be transformed by the renewal of your mind, that by testing you may discern what is the will of God, what is good and acceptable and perfect."

Romans 12:2 (ESV)

SOAP DEVOTIONS

Observation

_____
_____
_____
_____
_____

Application

_____
_____
_____
_____
_____
_____
_____

Prayer

_____
_____
_____
_____
_____
_____
_____

NAMING YOUR SHIELD

Finding Freedom Through Vulnerability

As human beings, we often develop protective personas that shield us from vulnerability and pain. These defense mechanisms serve as emotional armor but can hinder our growth and prevent us from experiencing true intimacy and connection. In this article, we will explore 20 protective personas we hide behind and discover how identifying and releasing these personas can lead to healing and freedom.

Then, we will explore the role of the limbic system in this process and the transformative power of new and opposite experiences. Let's take a look at the different types of protective personas that we tend to hide behind:

Take a look at the different types of protective personas that we tend to hide behind and check off the ones that resonate:

☐ **The Perfectionist:** Hiding behind a facade of perfection, we strive for flawlessness to avoid criticism and rejection.

☐ **The People-Pleaser:** We become overly focused on meeting others' expectations, sacrificing our needs and desires.

☐ **The Control Freak:** Seeking to maintain control, we micromanage every aspect of our lives to avoid uncertainty and vulnerability.

☐ **The Know-It-All:** We constantly need to prove our intelligence and expertise, fearing that admitting ignorance will diminish our worth.

☐ **The Victim:** We adopt a victim mentality, shifting responsibility onto others and avoiding personal accountability.

☐ **The Escapist:** We use various forms of escapism, such as excessive entertainment or substance abuse, to avoid facing reality and dealing with emotional pain.

☐ **The Pessimist:** We approach life with a negative outlook, anticipating the worst outcomes as an effort to protect ourselves from disappointment.

☐ **The Overachiever:** We relentlessly pursue success and accomplishments, believing our worth is tied to external achievements.

☐ **The Enabler:** We enable others' destructive behaviors or dependencies, seeking validation and avoiding confrontation.

☐ **The Martyr:** We sacrifice our own needs and desires for the sake of others, seeking validation through self-sacrifice.

☐ **The Comedian:** We use humor as a defense mechanism, deflecting vulnerability and masking our genuine emotions.

☐ **The Busybody:** We keep ourselves constantly busy, avoiding silence and solitude to distract from inner pain or unresolved issues.

☐ **The Ice Queen:** We distance ourselves emotionally from others, fearing rejection and protecting our hearts from potential hurt.

☐ **The People-Avoider:** We avoid our emotions by over-spiritualizing situations.

☐ **The Drama Queen:** We create or amplify drama, seeking attention and validation through chaotic situations.

☐ **The Procrastinator:** We delay taking action or making decisions, fearing failure or making the wrong choice.

☐ **The Daydreamer:** We disconnect from reality through excessive daydreaming, fantasizing, or living in a virtual world.

☐ **The Bully:** We protect ourselves by hurting others, often through making fun of others, coercing them to agree with you, or manipulating them to go along with you.

☐ **The Over-thinker:** We constantly overthink and overanalyze every situation, fearing making mistakes or facing potential consequences.

☐ **The Recluse:** We isolate ourselves from society, judging others' lifestyles, philosophies, and decisions.

Identifying and Releasing Protective Personas:

NOW THAT WE HAVE EXPLORED THESE PROTECTIVE PERSONAS REFLECT ON YOUR OWN LIFE. WHICH OF THESE PERSONAS RESONATE WITH YOU THE MOST?

1 _____

2 _____

3 _____

Recognizing and acknowledging these patterns is the first step towards releasing them.

IN WHAT SITUATIONS DO YOU FIND YOURSELF HIDING BEHIND THESE DEFENSE MECHANISMS?

_____

_____

_____

_____

_____

_____

_____

HOW HAVE THESE PROTECTIVE PERSONAS INFLUENCED YOUR RELATIONSHIPS AND PERSONAL GROWTH?

_____

_____

_____

_____

_____

_____

_____

_____

_____

_____

WHAT FEARS OR PAST EXPERIENCES MIGHT HAVE CONTRIBUTED TO DEVELOPING THESE DEFENSE MECHANISMS?

_____

_____

_____

_____

ARE THESE PROTECTIVE PERSONAS CURRENTLY POSITIVELY SERVING YOU? HOW MIGHT THEY BE HINDERING YOUR EMOTIONAL WELL-BEING AND RELATIONSHIPS?

_____

_____

_____

_____

_____

Understanding the Role of the Limbic System

Healing Through New Experiences

The limbic system, which plays a crucial role in our emotions and behaviors, can be deeply impacted by our protective personas. These defense mechanisms become deeply ingrained in our neural pathways, reinforcing patterns of thought and behavior.

However, healing comes through new and opposite experiences. By consciously challenging and stepping out of our comfort zones, we rewire our brains and create new pathways that foster growth and emotional well-being. Consider a hiking trail that has been walked repeatedly, making it the path of least resistance. It takes effort to step outside the path, but stepping off the path will be necessary if the worn path leads in a direction you don't want to go. Over time, you can imprint a new path that will become the new default. The same is true of your brain's neural networks, which control your subconscious decisions. You can change the path in your neural network by embracing vulnerability, seeking counseling, coaching, or therapy, and engaging in activities that allow you to experience new perspectives and interactions.

Releasing protective personas requires courage, self-reflection, and a willingness to embrace vulnerability. By identifying and acknowledging these defense mechanisms and how they hinder your growth, you create cognitive dissonance, which can propel change. By challenging ourselves and engaging in new experiences, we rewire our brains, fostering emotional growth and forging authentic connections.

May we have the courage to release the personas that hinder our true selves and step into a life of authenticity, courage, joy, and genuine connection with others.

WHAT STEP CAN YOU TAKE TO BEGIN REWIRING YOUR BRAIN'S NEURAL NETWORK IN A POSITIVE WAY?

_____

_____

_____

_____

_____

RESPONDING VS. REACTING

Cultivating Connection in the Face of Instinctual Triggers

As human beings, we possess instinctual survival responses known as *fight, flight, or freeze*. While these reactions serve us well in dangerous situations, they can hinder our ability to cultivate connection and understanding with those we love. This article will help you understand *reacting versus responding*, how to identify these instinctual triggers, and how to employ practical strategies to foster connection and growth in our relationships. Through self-exploration and personal development, we can discover the power of selecting deliberate responses — unlocking a world of compassion, empathy, and authentic connection.

Recognizing Reactivity:

Reacting is an instinctual reply to a threatening stimulus, often marked by fear, anger, or defensiveness. When faced with a perceived threat or conflict, our *fight, flight or freeze* response may be triggered, hindering our ability to communicate effectively and connect. It is essential to cultivate self-awareness to identify *reactive* patterns in ourselves. Notice **physical** cues such as increased heart rate, shallow breathing, a knotted stomach, a headache, or muscle tension. Recognize **emotional** signals such as irritability, defensiveness, or an overwhelming desire to escape the situation. Awareness of these signs allows us to pause, step back, and choose a more intentional response.

Choosing to Respond:

Responding, in contrast to *reacting*, involves consciously engaging thoughtfully and empathetically. It requires us to override our instinctual *reactions* and access higher cognitive functions to foster connection and understanding. To *respond* effectively, practice self-regulation techniques such as deep breathing, mindfulness, or taking a short break to regain composure. By creating a pause, we can detach ourselves from immediate emotional *reactions* and choose a *response* aligned with our values and priorities.

Active Listening and Empathy:

Active listening and empathy play a vital role in *responding* rather than *reacting*. When we truly listen and seek to understand our loved ones, we create an environment that fosters connection and mutual respect.

Engage in active listening by giving your full attention, maintaining eye contact, and providing verbal and nonverbal cues that demonstrate understanding and interest. Practice empathetic responses by acknowledging and validating your loved ones' emotions and experiences. Cultivate a mindset of genuine curiosity, seeking to understand their perspective and feelings without judgment.

Cultivating Emotional Intelligence:

Emotional intelligence is essential for responding effectively to instinctual triggers. It involves recognizing and managing our own emotions, while also empathizing with and seeking to understand the feelings of others. We can develop emotional intelligence by practicing self-reflection — identifying triggers and understanding how they affect our responses. As you do that, you'll cultivate self-compassion, which will position you to extend that compassion to others. Often, when we are critical and judgmental towards others, it stems from our harsh inner critic. We hold others to the impossible standard to which we hold ourselves. But when you begin to understand what has caused you pain and give yourself grace for the ways you are imperfect, you become more aware of the pain of others and more able to offer them the compassion they need, too.

In our relationships, the choice between reacting and responding can significantly impact our ability to connect, understand, and grow with those we love. By recognizing our instinctual *fight, flight, or freeze* reactions and consciously choosing to *respond*, we open the door to deeper connection and greater understanding.

Practice self-awareness, active listening, and empathy to foster meaningful dialogue and emotional validation. Cultivate emotional intelligence to navigate instinctual challenges with grace and compassion. Remember, by choosing to respond rather than *react*, we create opportunities for love, connection, and personal growth within our most cherished relationships.

Take time this week to observe how you are balancing your communication with others. Is there a need to go back and investigate what's under the surface in your life?

BLENDED FAMILIES

BY DEBBIE RASA

When family extends

beyond blood.

More from Debbie Rasa
(scan to watch)

DO YOU HAVE A BLENDED FAMILY?

If so, there's a good chance that you have experienced immense pain. Blended families are unique and bring unforeseen challenges that many are unaware of when they endeavor to join their families. However, blended families can also bring tremendous joy and restoration to the hearts of everyone in the family. In this article, we will acknowledge the challenges unique to blended families and offer an approach to help you navigate with care so you can cultivate peace and joy in your family.

While traditional families are not the only way to build a family, the loss of the nuclear family involves grief, whether from divorce, death, or abandonment. Regardless of the specific circumstances, parents and children often experience intense, long-lasting emotions that impact the whole family.

As a parent in a blended family, you may encounter feelings of anger, where you get impatient, critical, or frustrated. You may feel humiliated, leading you to withdraw or lash out. You may feel violated, disrespected, or dismissed. You may feel a sense of powerlessness and shame, leading to deep feelings of despair. All of these feelings are normal human emotions. Still, they tend to show up frequently when endeavoring to blend a family. It's imperative to keep in mind that when unaddressed and invalidated, any of these feelings can lead to loneliness and isolation -- for yourself and your children.

Children, especially once their mom or their dad gets remarried, and particularly if the other spouse has children as well, can experience an immense amount of fear. They often feel anxious, insecure, or threatened by the new step-parent or step-sibling(s). Suddenly, they are sharing their parent and space with others, which can be extremely difficult. It's normal for children in blended families to feel confused and experience ambivalent emotions, swinging on a pendulum as they figure out how to exist in their new reality. As the parent, it's important to remember that most children do not know how to name, express, or process these confusing feelings. Often, it comes out primarily as anger and anxiety. Unfortunately, our children frequently take out their negative emotions on themselves and their parents. They need their parents to model healthy emotional expression and regulation. You are responsible for providing your children the tools to navigate this challenging experience, but that doesn't mean it's all on you. With the help of others, like trained therapists, devoted mentors, and experienced friends, you can help your kids process and navigate the difficulty of a blended family. Most importantly, as you work to take care of yourself and learn to self-regulate, you'll be a safe space for your kids.

Aside from your kids, you may also experience many difficult emotions when dealing with ex-spouses -- yours and your partner's. Even when amicable, it can be challenging to co-parent. And when feelings are raw, it's common for hurtful things to be said and done. It is all very complex and often sensitive for everyone involved. And it takes immense patience, grace, and humility to navigate with care. Here are five fundamental approaches to consider when building a healthy blended family.

1. Patience and Understanding: Leading a blended family requires patience and understanding, as family dynamics can be complex. Recognize that each family member has a different perspective, experience, and emotional journey. Listen to and understand each family member's feelings and perspectives. Show empathy and create an environment where everyone feels heard and validated. You can validate someone's feelings and experience, even if you disagree with their perspective. This work to attune to them lays the groundwork for connecting and eventually offering a new perspective or helpful feedback. Patience and understanding will help build trust and foster a sense of unity within the blended family.

2. Communication and Open Dialogue: Effective communication is essential in a blended family. Establish open lines of communication where family members can express their thoughts, concerns, and needs openly and honestly. Encourage regular family meetings or discussions to address any challenges or conflicts, making space for family members to share if they are open. But keep in mind that it is counterproductive to force people to share if they are not ready. Rather, consider how that person feels most comfortable -- going for a walk, a drive, or an ice cream date. Clear and open communication will help resolve conflict and build strong relationships within the blended family.

3. Building a New Family Culture: Creating a new family culture that embraces unity and inclusivity is essential in a blended family. Encourage activities and traditions that involve all family members and help them bond. Establish new family rituals, such as weekly game nights, shared meals, or going to church together to create shared experiences that will strengthen the family bond. Involve all family members in decision-making to allow everyone to feel valued and included. Building a new family culture helps create a sense of belonging and unity among family members.

4. Consistency Over Time: Our spouses and children will watch what we do much closer than we think. Our words are put to the test by our actions and behaviors with consistency over time. I cannot overstate the value of consistency over time. We build trust through consistency over time. We show our family they can trust our sincerity, reliability, care, and competency through consistency over time. We must consistently show that we can avoid losing our temper, avoid shutting down, and move towards engagement with our families regularly and over a long period. Building trust takes time. And consistency. (Have I overstated it yet? I hope so!)

5. Don't Do it Alone: Don't try to have a blended family alone. If you have a blended family, you need others to support and pour into you. Find women who can speak into you with wisdom and sage advice from a biblical perspective grounded in Christ. Do your best to seek out the counsel and support of others with a blended family. We all need to walk closely with others, but this is especially true when dealing with the complexity and nuance of navigating a blended family.

Reflection

TAKE TIME TO JOURNAL ABOUT THE FEELINGS YOU'VE EXPERIENCED WHILE NAVIGATING A BLENDED FAMILY.

_____

_____

_____

_____

_____

_____

_____

WHAT DOES A HEALTHY BLENDED FAMILY LOOK LIKE TO YOU? DESCRIBE YOUR DREAM FOR YOUR NEW FAMILY.

_____

_____

_____

_____

_____

_____

_____

HOW DO YOU WANT EVERYONE WITHIN YOUR NEW FAMILY UNIT TO FEEL? HOW CAN YOU HELP SUPPORT AND CULTIVATE THAT?

_____

_____

_____

_____

_____

_____

_____

_____

_____

IF YOU HAVE A BLENDED FAMILY, WHO ARE SOME PEOPLE YOU CAN GATHER AROUND YOU TO SUPPORT YOU?

_____

_____

_____

_____

_____

_____

_____

IF YOU KNOW SOMEONE WITH A BLENDED FAMILY, HOW CAN YOU CONTACT THEM AND OFFER SUPPORT?

_____

_____

_____

_____

_____

_____

_____

_____

FINDING PEACE IN THE PRESENT

Learning to live in the present is crucial for our overall well-being in our often fast-paced and hectic lives. One of the most effective tools for training your body to be present is practicing grounding. Grounding techniques provide a practical and effective way to anchor ourselves in the present moment, helping us gain clarity, reduce anxiety, and enhance our overall mental and emotional resilience. This article will explore the importance of being present, the transformative practice of grounding, and the benefits of finding peace in the present. We will also introduce the 5-4-3-2-1 Grounding Technique and discuss incorporating grounding into everyday life.

Life often presents us with challenges and hardships that can overwhelm us. Grounding provides a space for reflection, allowing us to grieve losses, celebrate victories, and find balance. Being present and acknowledging our emotions opens the door to healing and growth. Grounding helps us navigate difficult times with greater clarity and resilience, enabling us to approach life's complexities with a renewed perspective.

This pivotal practice is not only about finding inner peace but also about connecting with God in the present moment so we can experience Him in the here and now. When we dwell on the past or worry about the future, we risk missing out on Christ's limitless peace in the present. Grounding allows us to connect with God in the present moment, fostering a deeper spiritual awareness and nourishing our faith journey.

Psalm 16:11 reminds us, "You make known to me the path of life; you will fill me with joy in your presence, with eternal pleasures at your right hand." By anchoring ourselves in the present, we create space to experience the fullness of God's joy and peace in our lives.

The 5-4-3-2-1 Grounding Technique

Begin this exercise by engaging your senses. Name five things you can see around you, four things you can touch, three things you can hear, two things you can smell, and one thing you can taste. This simple exercise redirects your focus from racing thoughts to the present moment, providing stability and grounding.

Engage and Name Your Senses

- 5 - see
- 4 - touch
- 3 - hear
- 2 - smell
- 1 - taste

After completing the grounding exercise, take a moment to reflect on how you feel. Do you notice a shift in your state of mind? Are you experiencing a greater sense of calm and clarity? Grounding allows us to escape the whirlwind of thoughts and emotions and reconnect with the present, fostering a greater sense of control and inner peace.

Grounding is not limited to specific moments of distress; we can incorporate it into our daily lives as a proactive practice for emotional well-being. By consciously being present and attuned to our senses, we train our brain and body to connect more with ourselves and the world around us. Regularly reflecting on our feelings without judgment, listening to our bodies, and engaging in self-care helps us stay grounded amid life's ups and downs.

Reflection

**TAKE ANOTHER MOMENT TO PRACTICE THE
5-4-3-2-1 GROUNDING TECHNIQUE AND REFLECT
ON THE EXPERIENCE. NOTE HOW YOU FEEL
NOW COMPARED TO MOMENTS BEFORE THE
GROUNDING EXERCISE.**

_____

_____

_____

_____

_____

_____

_____

_____

**WHEN COULD YOU INCORPORATE THIS
EXERCISE INTO YOUR DAILY LIFE?**

_____

_____

_____

_____

**WRITE A COMMITMENT TO YOURSELF FOR HOW
YOU WILL ENGAGE IN GROUNDING PRACTICES
FOR A MORE PRESENT LIFE.**

_____

_____

_____

_____

_____

ADVC

CATE

Let me tell you more about this
section, "ADVOCATE."
(scan to watch)

SOAP DEVOTIONS

Scripture

"Jesus called them together and said, 'You know that the rulers of the Gentiles lord it over them, and their high officials exercise authority over them. Not so with you. Instead, whoever wants to become great among you must be your servant, and whoever wants to be first must be your slave—just as the Son of Man did not come to be served, but to serve, and to give his life as a ransom for many.'"

Matthew 20:25-28

Application

Observation

Prayer

BEYOND EGO

Exploring the Nature of Selflessness in Leadership

In his acclaimed book Good to Great, Jim Collins delves into the characteristics distinguishing great companies from their average counterparts. One of the fundamental traits he uncovers is the presence of servant leadership — a concept that revolves around selflessness and a focus on the greater good. In this article, we will delve into the essence of selfless leadership, as outlined in Collins' work, and explore the potential pitfalls that leaders encounter when ego takes precedence. Additionally, we will provide practical points on embodying this principle in the workplace and at home.

In Good to Great, Collins introduces the concept of Level 5 Leadership, which incorporates a powerful blend of personal humility and unwavering professional will. Leaders channel their ambition and drive toward the success of the organization and its people rather than their personal gain. They prioritize collective interests over individual desires, making selflessness a cornerstone of their leadership approach.

Pitfalls of Ego-Centric Leadership

Ego-centric leadership can be detrimental to both leaders and the organizations they lead. When leaders become consumed by their egos, they tend to prioritize personal recognition and self-aggrandizement, often leading to toxic environments and poor decision-making. Some common pitfalls include:

1. Lack of Empathy: Egotistical leaders may disregard their team members' needs and concerns, leading to a breakdown in trust and communication.
2. Micromanagement: A leader focused on personal glory may micromanage their team, stifling creativity and innovation.
3. Resistance to Feedback: Ego-centric leaders may be unwilling to accept criticism or feedback, hindering personal and organizational growth.
4. Short-Term Thinking: Leaders driven by ego may prioritize quick wins and short-term gains, neglecting the organization's long-term vision.

Embodying Selflessness in the Workplace and Home

1. Lead by Example: Demonstrating selflessness starts with leaders themselves. In your actions and decisions, model humility, empathy, and a commitment to the greater good.
2. Foster a Culture of Trust: Build a culture of open communication and trust. Encourage feedback, listen actively, and value your team members' opinions.
3. Empower Others: Instead of controlling every aspect of a project, empower your team members by delegating responsibilities and giving them the autonomy to excel.
4. Recognize and Celebrate Team Achievements: Shift the focus from individual recognition to celebrating team accomplishments. Boost morale and motivation by acknowledging your team members' contributions.
5. Embrace a Long-Term Vision: Develop and communicate a compelling vision for the organization's future. Show dedication to its realization, even if it means sacrifices in the short term.
6. Practice Active Listening: In professional and personal settings, actively listen to others without interrupting or judging. Seek to understand their perspectives and concerns.
7. Balance Work and Personal Life: Encourage work-life balance among your team members and practice it yourself. A well-rounded, fulfilled leader can better serve others.

The essence of selfless leadership, as described by Collins, lies in the ability to put the needs of others before one's own. Ego-centric leadership can hinder the growth and success of both leaders and organizations. By embracing humility, empathy, and a focus on the greater good, leaders can foster an environment of trust and collaboration. Applying these principles in the workplace and home can create positive impact, ultimately leading to lasting success and fulfillment for all involved.

Reflection

HOW HAVE YOU OPERATED FROM AN EGO-CENTRIC PERSPECTIVE IN THE SPACES WHERE YOU LEAD?

_____

_____

_____

_____

_____

_____

WHAT ARE SOME PRACTICAL WAYS YOU CAN EMBODY SERVANT LEADERSHIP IN YOUR WORKPLACE?

_____

_____

_____

_____

_____

WHAT ARE SOME PRACTICAL WAYS YOU CAN EMBODY SERVANT LEADERSHIP IN YOUR HOME?

_____

_____

_____

_____

_____

_____

SOAP DEVOTIONS

Scripture

When he had finished washing their feet, he put on his clothes and returned to his place. "Do you understand what I have done for you?" he asked them. "You call me 'Teacher' and 'Lord,' and rightly so, for that is what I am. Now that I, your Lord and Teacher, have washed your feet, you also should wash one another's feet. I have set you an example that you should do as I have done for you. Very truly I tell you, no servant is greater than his master, nor is a messenger greater than the one who sent him. Now that you know these things, you will be blessed if you do them.

John 13:12-17 (NIV)

Application

Observation

Prayer

GOOD BOUNDARIES

Protecting the Internal &

Empowering the External

In a world that often demands from us in excess—our time, energy, and resources—women must understand and practice the art of setting boundaries. This article will explore the significance of good internal and external boundaries, illuminating how they protect and empower us to lead healthier, more balanced lives. Through understanding and implementing these boundaries, we can become better leaders in our families and communities, fostering environments where creativity, growth, and authentic generosity flourish.

UNDERSTANDING BOUNDARIES

Internal Boundaries: *The Leadership Within*

Internal boundaries relate to how we manage ourselves—our thoughts, emotions, and actions. They are the personal guidelines we set that dictate how we interact with our inner world, influencing our self-esteem, identity, emotional regulation, and decision-making processes.

Let's go deeper:

1. Reflect on a moment when you were overwhelmed by emotions. Did you shut down the feelings or let them dictate your actions? Or were you able to navigate through them non-judgmentally with self-compassion and understanding?
2. Consider your thoughts and self-talk. Do they tend to lean more nurturing or critical? How does this affect your daily life?

External Boundaries: *Navigating Relationships*

External boundaries define how we interact with the world around us. They help us communicate our personal or professional needs, limits, and expectations in our relationships, fostering mutual understanding and respect. These are where we define where we end, and someone else begins.

Let's go deeper:

THINK ABOUT A TIME WHEN SOMEONE ASKED TOO MUCH OF YOU. DID YOU FIND A WAY TO SET A BOUNDARY? IF NOT, WHAT HINDERED YOU? WHAT CONSEQUENCES DID YOU SUBSEQUENTLY FACE? IF SO, WHAT WAS THAT EXPERIENCE LIKE FOR YOU?

_____

_____

_____

_____

RECALL A SITUATION WHERE YOU FELT RESPECTED AND UNDERSTOOD BY OTHERS. WHAT BOUNDARIES HAD YOU COMMUNICATED THAT CONTRIBUTED TO THIS FEELING?

_____

_____

_____

RECALL A SITUATION WHERE YOU FELT RESPECTED AND UNDERSTOOD BY OTHERS. WHAT BOUNDARIES HAD YOU COMMUNICATED THAT CONTRIBUTED TO THIS FEELING?

_____

_____

_____

_____

BENEFITS OF BOUNDARIES

Good Boundaries: *Protect*

Good boundaries protect our well-being, enable us to recharge, and ultimately give to others without depleting ourselves. When we name and communicate our natural limitations to others, we are protected from overextending beyond our capacity. By protecting ourselves through honoring our boundaries, we prevent the resentment of feeling taken advantage of. As a result, we can enjoy more fulfilling and respectful relationships. It is also important to note that often, the places we struggle most to hold boundaries are the places we've been wounded. It can feel incredibly vulnerable to maintain a boundary in an area where we've been hurt in the past. And often, we are blind to the areas in which we struggle to hold boundaries because our painful past has led us to believe that holding a boundary is not an option. Communicating our boundaries and having them respected fosters safety in relationships.

Let's go deeper:

WHEN HAVE YOU FELT YOUR BEST, BOTH EMOTIONALLY AND PHYSICALLY? WERE THERE CLEAR BOUNDARIES IN PLACE THAT CONTRIBUTED TO THIS STATE?

_____

_____

_____

CAN YOU REMEMBER A TIME WHEN YOU FELT UNSAFE? CONSIDER HOW A BOUNDARY MAY HAVE BEEN BREACHED. HOW HAS THAT IMPACTED HOW YOU HOLD BOUNDARIES TODAY?

_____

_____

_____

Good Boundaries: *Empower*

Protective boundaries empower us to lead by example, model self-respect, and give joyfully. Modeling a life of keeping boundaries allows you to effectively lead others in your family and community, ultimately advocating for healthy relationships and interactions for everyone. Moreover, a byproduct of protecting ourselves through keeping boundaries is holding onto a sense of agency over when and how we choose to give of ourselves. That allows us to give to others with a sense of authenticity and generosity rather than obligation, which leads to resentment.

Boundaries empower us to live lives marked by joy!

Let's go deeper:

CONSIDER A LEADER YOU ADMIRE FOR THEIR ABILITY TO MAINTAIN BALANCE AND RESPECT IN THEIR INTERACTIONS. WHAT BOUNDARIES DO YOU OBSERVE THEM IMPLEMENTING?

_____

_____

_____

_____

HOW DO BOUNDARIES (OR THE LACK THEREOF) CURRENTLY AFFECT YOUR ABILITY TO BE CREATIVE, GROW, AND GIVE AUTHENTICALLY?

_____

_____

_____

_____

Reflecting on our experiences with good and bad boundaries can provide valuable insights into improving our relationships with others.

Setting and respecting boundaries is **not about building walls** but about **bridging gaps** between our inner needs and outer expressions. It's a delicate balance that requires constant attention and adjustment (made easier by the practice of being present!). With practice, we can master this art, leading to a life that's not only healthier for us but also enriching and inspiring for those around us.

As you contemplate these questions and reflect on your own boundary experiences, remember that it's always possible to start setting healthy boundaries. It's never too late to make a change. While it is normal to have some anxiety and hesitation around setting new boundaries, especially with those you love and in environments where there is much at stake (like work), your health is worth it. Each step towards understanding and implementing good boundaries leads to a more balanced, empowered, and authentic life.

AUTHENTIC LEADERSHIP

Did you know that our bodies can sense at a neurological level whether someone is being authentic with us? We have a system called the Enteric Nervous System that senses, perceives, and judges our surroundings at a subconscious level. It's why sometimes you're with someone and things feel off, but you can't quite put words to it. It's why sometimes you walk into a room and immediately tense up and feel uncomfortable. Our bodies innately know how to intuit authenticity. And so, if you want to be an effective leader, you must do the work to lead with authenticity.

Authentic leadership starts within. It begins with diving deep into your inner world, past trauma, and childhood wounds. It requires you to be honest as you become aware of your true thoughts, feelings, and experiences and practice applying grace to your inner life. Without doing this work, others can sense the incongruence between what you say and what they perceive, leading to a lack of trust. And if people don't trust you, you cannot be an effective leader.

At a high level, this is how you become an authentic leader:

1. Awareness
2. Truth
3. Compassion
4. Vulnerability
5. Accountability

Let's Go Deeper

Awareness
The beauty of the Enteric Nervous System is that it perceives what is true at a subconscious level. In this way, it protects us from harm. It is aware of what we cannot yet see. But if we want to live authentically, we have to become aware. The first step towards authenticity is accepting that you must become aware.

Truth
Honesty is the foundation of trust, and this is especially true for those in leadership. But it's not just about "telling the truth." It begins much deeper. It begins within. You must start by being honest with yourself about your experiences, thoughts, and feelings. It may feel scary to honestly acknowledge what is real, but the next step will help you move forward with grace and compassion.

Compassion
Compassion is defined as "deep awareness of the suffering of another, coupled with the wish to relieve it." But what we want to invite you to at this point is self-compassion. As you honestly acknowledge your thoughts and feelings, you may notice judgmental thoughts followed by feelings of shame. Often, we have avoided and dismissed our true thoughts and emotions because we fear the rejection, guilt, and shame that may accompany them. But if you want to lead authentically, you must be honest. To process the truth of your feelings and thoughts, you will need to treat yourself with compassion. Consider how you would respond to a dear friend experiencing the thoughts and feelings you now acknowledge in yourself. How would you treat them? What would you say to them? We can often learn how to have self-compassion by applying how we treat loved ones to how we treat ourselves.

Vulnerability

Vulnerability and shame researcher Brene Brown says, "Vulnerability is based on mutuality and requires boundaries and trust. It's not oversharing, purging, indiscriminate disclosure, or celebrity-style social media information dumps. Vulnerability is about sharing our feelings and our experiences with people who have earned the right to hear them." This is the next step in authentic leadership. Now that you've become aware and honest about your thoughts and feelings and have begun to practice self-compassion, you need to find someone you can trust and share with them. Vulnerability takes courage, but it is essential for an authentic and meaningful life.

Accountability

Accountability acknowledges that you cannot do it alone. We need one another, and we need God's help. To live with accountability, we need to invite others to have a say in our lives. In our faith, this means using scripture to guide your life with wisdom. In our relationships, this means giving a few people in your life permission to ask hard questions and tell you when they sense something is off.

REFLECTION:

AWARENESS: TAKE A MOMENT TO SEARCH WITHIN YOURSELF AND BECOME AWARE OF WHAT HAS BEEN HIDDEN.

_____

_____

_____

_____

VULNERABILITY: WHO CAN YOU SHARE WITH?

_____

_____

_____

_____

TRUTH: WHAT THOUGHTS AND FEELINGS DO YOU NEED TO BE HONEST WITH YOURSELF ABOUT?

_____

_____

_____

_____

ACCOUNTABILITY: HOW WILL YOU COMMIT TO ACCOUNTABILITY?

_____

_____

_____

_____

COMPASSION: WRITE A COMPASSIONATE, NON-JUDGMENTAL NOTE TO YOURSELF.

_____

_____

_____

_____

WHICH OF THESE 5 IS MOST DIFFICULT FOR YOU? WHY?

_____

_____

_____

_____

YOUR STORY

Serving Others with Your Story

Serving others is the pinnacle of leadership. Your work in this journal to learn and process your story is foundational for leading others. You should be so proud of yourself! The final step of this process is learning to share your story with others.

Think back to the most impactful moments in your life. You will likely notice that the times you were most transformed by an expression of leadership were when someone was vulnerable enough to lead through their story of trials and triumphs. Stories are how we connect with others. Our stories make us real to others. And it's our stories that have the potential to inspire others.

We detract from our leadership potential when we hide the foundational moments that shaped us into who we are today—the good, the bad, and the ugly.

After all, who wants a cookie-cutter leader parroting cliche growth strategies? What people desire most in our families, workplaces, and the world around us is grounded guidance from authentic people.

One way to better understand how to lead through your story is to write your life story out in the third person and read it back to yourself or even share it with a safe person. This vantage point helps us as leaders empathetically connect with our humanity and create moments of reflection. Writing your story gives you a more profound sense of your resiliency. It also highlights the strategies that have and have not worked for you, giving you more tools to advocate for others.

Lastly, writing your story lets you connect with the emotions associated with your memories. When we can embody those emotions in a safe space, we are able to integrate them healthily, making the memories less emotionally charged and giving us more agency over how we share our stories with others.

As a conclusion of this reflective journey, we encourage you to write your story. Grab a journal (or use the pages provided here) and start at the beginning. Feel free to be creative, but also be sure to say what you need to say with honesty. This exploration is for you. It's not a public forum; instead, it's a glimpse into how your unique story can be used to encourage someone else.

It's important to note that along the way, you may discover aspects of your story that you are still grieving, struggling with, or need support for. There is no better leadership preparation than taking the time to heal and grow in the places of our story that are still raw and unrefined. Being in process doesn't necessarily disqualify us from leading others; instead, it illuminates areas where we can get stronger and more courageously vulnerable in a healthy way. Ultimately, this expands our ability to walk with others right where they are - because we are still in process, too!

Remember, you are not alone, and your story is not over. "We have overcome by the blood of the lamb and the word of our testimony!"
Revelation 12:11

VISIT OUR WEBSITE

LiveLifeUnplugged.org

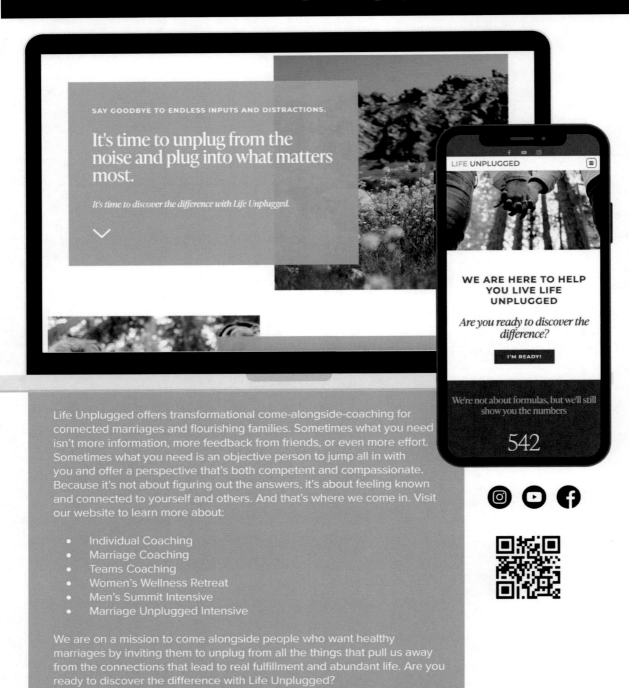

SAY GOODBYE TO ENDLESS INPUTS AND DISTRACTIONS.

It's time to unplug from the noise and plug into what matters most.

It's time to discover the difference with Life Unplugged.

LIFE UNPLUGGED

WE ARE HERE TO HELP YOU LIVE LIFE UNPLUGGED

Are you ready to discover the difference?

I'M READY!

We're not about formulas, but we'll still show you the numbers

542

Life Unplugged offers transformational come-alongside-coaching for connected marriages and flourishing families. Sometimes what you need isn't more information, more feedback from friends, or even more effort. Sometimes what you need is an objective person to jump all in with you and offer a perspective that's both competent and compassionate. Because it's not about figuring out the answers, it's about feeling known and connected to yourself and others. And that's where we come in. Visit our website to learn more about:

- Individual Coaching
- Marriage Coaching
- Teams Coaching
- Women's Wellness Retreat
- Men's Summit Intensive
- Marriage Unplugged Intensive

We are on a mission to come alongside people who want healthy marriages by inviting them to unplug from all the things that pull us away from the connections that lead to real fulfillment and abundant life. Are you ready to discover the difference with Life Unplugged?

Marriage Health
with
James & Teri Craft

If you are fighting for your marriage, don't face this fight alone. We want to help you fight issues you face in your marriage when it comes to communication, intimacy, conflict, or if you're just fighting to fall back in love with your partner. With backgrounds in therapy and coaching, we'll use everything within our toolkit to help your marriage find health. A healthy marriage starts with a healthy you.

"Saving Your Marriage Can't Happen Alone."

PARTNER WITH US

Ready to help others discover the difference with Life Unplugged?

Your benevolent partnership is changing lives. Marriages are deepening.
Men are recovering. Women are healing. Families are flourishing.
And your generosity is helping to make it happen. Thank you for joining us
in our mission to help more people discover the difference!

You've discovered the difference. And now you can make a difference.

Made in the USA
Las Vegas, NV
12 February 2025

18087207R00050

It all started with an implosion in our marriage that caused us to make a choice. We could accept the brokenness in front of us and move on — away from one another. Or we could endeavor to build something new — something more like the relationship we both wanted deep down. We desperately wanted to find a way to stay together. So we chose to rebuild.

But we quickly realized that trying to do it alone was like trying to operate on yourself -- maybe technically possible, but unwise, painful, and likely dangerous. We needed people to come alongside us to offer perspective, support, and encouragement to keep going. Thankfully, we were quickly surrounded. Those people helped to make the work we put in exponentially more impactful. And because these come-alongsiders were so crucial to our own journey, we began a quest to offer the same to others. Sharing what we'd been given. Coming alongside others as they put in the work. Helping people navigate their own journeys towards richer relationships and flourishing families.

Your marriage is between you and your spouse, but inviting others to come alongside you through the lows, plateaus, and eventual highs will allow it to thrive in ways you've only dreamed.

We are on a mission to come alongside you so you'll never have to struggle in isolation again.

LIVELIFEUNPLUGGED.ORG

9 798986 030975